P9-DDR-653

Looking for The Gulf Motel

PITT POETRY SERIES
ED OCHESTER, EDITOR

Looking for The Gulf Motel

Richard Blanco

UNIVERSITY OF PITTSBURGH PRESS

Published by the University of Pittsburgh Press, Pittsburgh, Pa., 15260
Copyright © 2012, Richard Blanco
All rights reserved
Manufactured in the United States of America
Printed on acid-free paper

10 9 8 7 6 5 4 3 2 1

ISBN 13: 978-0-8229-6201-4
ISBN 10: 0-8229-6201-2

For Geysa Claudia Valdés, *madre hay una sóla*

Contents

Looking for The Gulf Motel

Looking for The Gulf Motel
Marco Island, Florida

There should be nothing here I don't remember . . .

The Gulf Motel with mermaid lampposts
and ship's wheel in the lobby should still be
rising out of the sand like a cake decoration.
My brother and I should still be pretending
we don't know our parents, embarrassing us
as they roll the luggage cart past the front desk
loaded with our scruffy suitcases, two-dozen
loaves of Cuban bread, brown bags bulging
with enough mangos to last the entire week,
our espresso pot, the pressure cooker—and
a pork roast reeking garlic through the lobby.
All because we can't afford to eat out, not even
on vacation, only two hours from our home
in Miami, but far enough away to be thrilled
by *whiter* sands on the *west* coast of Florida,
where I should still be for the first time watching
the sun set instead of rise over the ocean.

There should be nothing here I don't remember . . .

My mother should still be in the kitchenette
of The Gulf Motel, her daisy sandals from Kmart
squeaking across the linoleum, still gorgeous
in her teal swimsuit and amber earrings
stirring a pot of *arroz-con-pollo*, adding sprinkles
of onion powder and dollops of tomato sauce.
My father should still be in a terrycloth jacket

smoking, clinking a glass of amber whiskey
in the sunset at the Gulf Motel, watching us
dive into the pool, two boys he'll never see
grow into men who will be proud of him.

There should be nothing here I don't remember . . .

My brother and I should still be playing *Parcheesi*,
my father should still be alive, slow dancing
with my mother on the sliding-glass balcony
of The Gulf Motel. No music, only the waves
keeping time, a song only their minds hear
ten-thousand nights back to their life in Cuba.
My mother's face should still be resting against
his bare chest like the moon resting on the sea,
the stars should still be turning around them.

There should be nothing here I don't remember . . .

My brother should still be thirteen, sneaking
rum in the bathroom, sculpting naked women
from sand. I should still be eight years old
dazzled by seashells and how many seconds
I hold my breath underwater—but I'm not.
I am thirty-eight, driving up Collier Boulevard,
looking for The Gulf Motel, for everything
that should still be, but isn't. I want to blame
the condos, their shadows for ruining the beach
and my past, I want to chase the snowbirds away

with their tacky mansions and yachts, I want
to turn the golf courses back into mangroves,
I want to find The Gulf Motel exactly as it was
and pretend for a moment, nothing lost is lost.

The Name I Wanted:

Not Ricardo but Richard, because I felt
like Richard Burton—a true Anglo-Saxon
in tights reciting lines from Othello, because
I wanted to be as handsome as Richard Gere
in a white tuxedo, because I had a pinky ring
just like Richard Dawson on *Family Feud*,
because I knew I could be just as wholesome
as Richie Cunningham, just as American
as my father's favorite president, Nixon.

Richard—not Ricardo, not my nicknames:
El Negrito—Little Black Boy—for my skin
the color of dry tobacco when I was born,
or *El Gallegito*—the Little Galician, because
that's what Tía Noelia called anyone like me
born in Spain, not a hundred percent Cuban.
Not *Rico*, the name Lupe wrote on my desk
branding me as Barry Manilow's Latin lover
in ruffled sleeves dancing conga at the *Copa,
Copa Cabana* all of eighth grade. And definitely
not *Ricardito*—Little Ricky—worse than Dick.

Richard—descendant of British royals, not
the shepherds of my mother's family, not
the plantain farmers on my father's side.
Richard—name of German composers, not
the swish of machetes, rapping of bongos.
Richard—more elegant than my grandfather
in his polyester suit, Chiclets in his pocket,

more refined than my grandmother gnawing
mangos, passing gas at the kitchen sink.

Ricardo De Jesús Blanco, I dub thee myself
        Sir Richard Jesus White
defender of my own country, protector
of my wishes, conqueror of mirrors, sovereign
of my imagination—a name for my name.

My grandmother was the bookie, set up
at the kitchen table that night, her hair
in curlers, pencil and pad jotting down
two-dollar bets, paying five-to-one
on which Miss would take the crown.

Abuelo put his money on Miss Wyoming—
She's got great teeth, he pronounced as if
complimenting a horse, not her smile
filling the camera before she wisped away
like a cloud in her creamy chiffon dress.

I dug up enough change from the sofa
and car seats to bet on Miss Wisconsin,
thinking I was as American as she because
I was as blond as she was, and I knew
that's where all the cheese came from.

That wasn't all: chocolate was from Miss
Pennsylvania, the capital of Miss Montana
was Helena, Mount Rushmore was in
Miss South Dakota, and I knew how to say
Miss *Con-nec-ti-cut,* unlike my Tía Gloria

who just pointed at the TV: *Esa—that one,*
claiming she had her same figure before
leaving Cuba. *It's true . . . I have pictures,*
she declared before cramming another
bocadito sandwich into her mouth.

Papá refused to bet on any of the Misses
because *Americanas all have skinny butts,*
he complained. *There's nothing like a big
culo cubano.* Everyone agreed—*es verdad*—
except for me and my little cousin Julito,

who apparently was a breast man at five,
reaching for Miss Alabama's bosom
on the screen, the leggy *mulata* sashaying
in pumps, swimsuit, seducing Tío Pedro
into picking her as the sure winner.

She's the one! She looks Cubana, he swore,
and she did, but she cost him five bucks.
¡Cojones! he exploded as confetti rained,
Bert Parks leading Miss Ohio, the new
Miss America, by the hand to the runway.

Gloves up to her elbows, velvet down
to her feet, crying diamonds into her bouquet,
the queen of *our* country, *our* land of the free,
amid the purple mountains of her majesty
floating across the stage, our living room,

though no one bet on her, and none of us
—not even me—could answer Mamá
when she asked: *¿Dónde está Ohio?*

Florida, the house we went to every Sunday, the house on a cul-de-sac of polite *americanos* just like her husband, the house where she was a *missus* instead of a *señora*, Johnson instead of Gómez, not my *tía* but my aunt in pink house slippers, an embroidered housecoat, reading *Good Housekeeping* with a gardenia tucked behind her ear, the house with a flower garden, not chickens like ours scratching through the backyard dirt, the house shaded by live oaks, not our sickly *mamey* trees half as big as the ones my father grew in Cuba, the house with a carport, her silver-dollar Buick, not our old Nova rusting in the rain, the house with two front doors, a castle, a magical doorbell that chimed "Jingle Bells" at Christmastime, *The Brady Bunch* house with an orange kitchen, an oven built into the wall, an upside-down fridge, bottom always filled with ice-cream sandwiches and Kool-Aid popsicles, the house of mac-n-cheese and blueberry pie, not *arroz-con-frijoles* and flan, the house of crayons and glitter she kept for me in a gold cigar box, the house where I saw myself in the polished coffee table with a crystal candy dish always filled with chocolate kisses, the house where we could sit in the living room, watch TV from her red-velvet sofa not covered in plastic like ours, the house of Sonny and Cher and Lawrence Welk on Sunday nights, not my mother's *telenovelas* or my grandfather's Westerns dubbed-over in Spanish, the house that spoke English, the house where I wasn't Cuban anymore, the house without a *revolución*, the house in one country, not two, the house that disappeared when she moved to Jersey, the house we never went to again, the house I never left.

Por favor Consuelo, play something—for la familia, her mother begged until she stomped to the bench, bored us with some waltz. I asked for *Crocodile Rock*, but she didn't know it (or so she said), hammered out a mambo instead, her waist-long hair swaying like a metronome keeping tempo and everyone two-three-fouring around the coffee table. I asked for *Muskrat Love*, but she kept the frenzy going with a *paso doble* setting off a chorus of ¡Olé! ¡Olé! ¡Olé! ringside at a bullfight tossing out roses. *Margaritaville,* I pleaded, but she followed with the sweet and slow honey of a bolero. *Okay, one more—that's it!* she warned. I yelled for *American Pie,* but the crowd demanded *¡Guantanamera!* that damn song about Cuba they all knew by heart. *¡Guantanamera!* My mother slapped my fingers out of my ears, made me sit on my hands. I had to listen to my grandmother caterwaul, dabbing the corners of her eyes, her voice cracking over a country I didn't know yet had to love like Tía Miri did, singing about *el campo* I never saw yet had to feel in Brenda's notes rising into mountains, resting in valleys, the click of her nail-tips on the keys like rain falling in the room, on my father. I had to watch him sink into the sofa, clutch his whiskey, follow her fingers rippling left, right. I had to sing with him like a *real* Cuban, had to feel displaced, broken, beautiful— and clap for more, had to make Consuelo play *Guantanamera* twice, three times, until she stuffed the sheet music back into the bench, marched to her room, leaving us and the piano a dumb black box without her.

Taking My Cousin's Photo at the Statue of Liberty
for Roxana

May she never miss the sun or the rain in the valley
trickling from Royal palms, or the plush red earth,
or the flutter of sugarcane fields and poincianas, or
the endless hem of turquoise sea around the island,
may she never remember the sea or her life again
in Cuba selling glossy postcards of the revolution
and *El Che* to sweaty Germans, may she never forget
the broken toilet and peeling stucco of her room
in a government-partitioned mansion dissolving
like a sand castle back into the Bay of Cienfuegos,
may she never have to count the dollars we'd send
for her wedding dress, or save egg rations for a cake,
may she be as American as I wanted to be once, in love
with its rosy-cheeked men in breeches and white wigs,
with the calligraphy of our *Liberty and Justice for All*,
our *We The People*, may she memorize all fifty states,
our rivers and mountains, sing "God Bless America"
like she means it, like she's never lived anywhere
else but here, may she admire our wars and our men
on the moon, may she believe our infomercials, buy
designer perfumes and underwear, drink Starbucks,
drive a Humvee, and have a dream, may she never
doubt America, may this be her country more than
it is mine when she lifts her Diet Coke like a torch
into the June sky and clutches her faux Chanel purse
to her chest, may she look into New York Harbor
for the rest of her life and hold still when I say, *Smile.*

Of Consequence, Inconsequently

A bearded shepherd in a gray wool vest,
a beret lowered to his brow, that's how
my blood has always imagined the man
who was my great-grandfather, his eyes
hazel, I was told once. But I'll never see

what he saw of his life in the cold rivers
of Asturias. I can only imagine the fog
caressing the hills of his village and him
watching from the window of the train
he took to Sevilla—*for love,* my mother
explained to me once, holding a ghost

of him in a photo on his wedding day
with an ascot tie and buttoned shoes
standing in a room filled with mahogany
and red roses. *Were* they red? What color
were the tiers of Spanish lace cascading
from my great-grandmother's dress?

Nothing can speak for them now, tell me
what they saw in their eyes that morning
they left for love or war or both, crossing
the sea to Cuban palms and cane fields
quietly sweetening under the quiet sun.
But what if they'd never met, what color

would my eyes be? Who would I be now
had they gone to Johannesburg instead,

or Maracaibo, or not left Sevilla at all?
Into what seas would I have cast thoughts,
what other cities would I've drowned in?

The countries I would've lost, or betrayed,
the languages I would speak or not speak,
the names that would've been my names—
I'd like to believe I've willed every detail
of my life, but I'm a consequence, a drop
of rain, a seed fallen by chance, here

in the middle of a story I don't know,
having to finish it and call it my own.

The Island Within
for Ruth Behar

I'm still thinking about your porch light
like a full moon casting a foggy halo
in the frigid air last night, the bare oaks
branching into the sky like nerve endings
inches away from the frozen stars,
the pink gables of your Victorian home
protesting yet another winter for you
captive in Ann Arbor as you practice
mambo by the fireplace. I'm following
your red-velvet shoes to conga beats
and bongo taps taking your body, but
not your life, from the snow mantling
your windows outside, 1,600 miles
away from Cuba. I'm tasting the *cafecito*
you made, the slice of homemade flan
floating in burnt sugar like the stories
you told me you can't finish writing,
no matter how many times you travel
through time back to Havana to steal
every memory ever stolen from you.

You're a thief anyone would forgive,
wanting only to imagine faces for names
chiseled on the graves of your family
at Guanabacoa, walk on Calle Aguacate
and pretend to meet the grandfather
you never met at his lace shop for lunch,
or pray the Kaddish like your mother
at the synagogue in El Vedado, stand

on the steps there like you once did
in a photo you can't remember taking.
I confess I pitied you, still trying to reach
that unreachable island within the island
you still call home. I thought I was done
with Cuba, tired of filling in the blanks,
but now I'm not sure. Maybe if I return
just once more, walk the sugarcane fields
my father once cut, drive down the road
where my mother once peddled guavas
to pay for textbooks, sit on the porch
of my grandmother's house, imagine her
still in the kitchen making *arroz-con-leche*—
maybe then I'll have an answer for you
last night when you asked me: *Would you
move to Cuba? Would you die there?*

Poem Between Havana and Varadero

Cousin Tino's never gone sixty, now
he's pushing ninety in a rented Kia,
first time driving automatic—a honk,
a grin as he dusts a Soviet Lada, '71,
same as his *other* car, puttering down

this road that shouldn't feel as right
as it does: windows down, radio up
blaring *real salsa*, my cousin JL playing
conga on the dash, a cig from his lips.
We click beers—*Viva Cuba*—though

I want to believe I'd hate my life here—
like Tino damning *la revolución de mierda*
under his breath as we pass the guards
at a control point staring him down—
but I can't, even as I read past the haunt

of El Che on billboards spelling out
my fate here: SOCIALISMO O MUERTE.
I don't want to forget I'm from someplace
else, but I do, unlike my brother listening
to AC/DC on his iPod, Facebooking

his post-divorce girlfriend, unmoved
by the mountains in the distance where
he was born, not me. Why should I be
the one to feel for this island, loathe
the German tourists at the rest stop

who drink *my* daiquiris, dance *mi salsa*
as if they're stomping out a campfire?
Terrible dancers, but what chutzpah,
just like JL ordering Tino to pull over
or he'll piss out the window. He stops

by a cove and JL searches for a bush.
I climb to a rocky ledge over the sea.
Beautiful, verdad? he yells back to me,
but the last thing I need is to love
this crocodile-shaped island that was

my beginning with no end, I don't want
to taste the waves shattering drops
on my lips nor hear Cuba speak through
the wind gusting up words in my ear:
  . . . *aquí eres el otro* . . .
      . . . *here you are the other* . . .
  . . . *eres viento y ola y tierra* . . .
      . . . *you are wind and wave and earth* . . .

JL zips up—*Vámonos*—he pronounces,
we get back in the Kia, back on the road
heading somewhere west of Varadero—
east of Havana—chased by a poem:
  . . . *aquí eres el que nunca fuistes* . .
      . . . *here you are who you never were* . . .
  . . . *eres viento y ola y tierra* . . .
      . . . *you are wind and wave and earth* . . .

Aquí eres el otro nieto, no se te olvida
el nombre de tu abuelo, ni sus cuentos entre
los naranjales, el perfume de las gardenias
en el jardín de tu abuela, sus ojos claros
como ópalos que ves en el oscuro de tus ojos.

        Here you are the other grandson, you don't forget
        your grandfather's name nor his stories among
        the orange groves, the perfume of the gardenias
        in your grandmother's garden, her hazel eyes
        like opals you see in the dark of your eyes.

Aquí eres el otro hijo, conoces tu madre
como niña barriendo su piso de tierra,
y tu padre cortando caña, bañándose
en las zanjas del valle, eres monte
entre los montes, una décima entre guajiros,
ola entre olas que nunca llegó a otra orilla.

        Here you are the other son, you know your mother
        as a girl sweeping the dirt floor of her home
        and your father cutting sugarcane, swimming
        in the valley swales, you are a mountain
        among the mountains, a *décima* among *guajiros,*
        a wave among waves that never reached another shore.

Aquí eres aquél aburrido de los chismes
de la lluvia, acostumbrado a los gritos
de los cañaverales en llamas, cansado
del cielo vestido de estrellas como lentejuelas
aquí, donde eres el que nunca fuistes,
el otro, nunca traducido, invisible.

        Here you are the one bored with gossip
        from the rain, accustomed to the screams

of sugarcane fields set ablaze, tired
of the sky dressed in stars like sequins
here, where you are who you never were,
the other, never translated, invisible.

Aquí eres nativo, andando, nunca perdido
entre estos trillitos de tierra hasta el ayer,
dejado huellas que no levanta ni borra
el viento entre tus dedos, entre las palmas,
siguiendo el susurro con los ojos cerrados.

Here you are native, wandering, never lost
through these dirt paths reaching yesterdays
leaving footprints not lifted or erased
by the wind through your fingers, the palms,
following their rustle with eyes closed.

The roosters' crows travel like gossip
from field to field, reaching the window
which is a painting of a tamarind tree
holding a three-quarter moon like a fruit
in its branches, their shadows sweeping
silently across the wall and the tile floor.
An invisible dog yowls, a tractor moans
in the distance, figurines on the shelves
from a faraway place named China turn
and stare at me listening to the far voice
of my Tío Sergio repeating in my mind:

I have nothing I want, but everything I need . . .
I have nothing I want, but everything I need . . .

Before dawn, it's easier to believe him
needing only what survived his death:
a black-and-white TV set, six white shirts
starched in the closet, his '71 Moskvich,
a gift from the Soviets for his loyalty
rusting in the yard, and a photo of Fidel
striking his fist on a podium, hanging
above his rocking chair absolutely still,
holding the space he once filled for hours
with stories of the struggle, *la revolución*:

I have nothing I want, but everything I need . . .
I have nothing I want, but everything I need . . .

The last perfume of the night jasmine
wanders in like an invisible woman,
this cup of *café-con-leche* in my hands
steams my face, and this bare light
barely shines on these blank walls,
convincing me for a moment everything
I need is in this room if I had the faith
of the palms and stalks of sugarcane
swaying blindly in the nightwinds,
of the mountains asleep in silhouette,
the chorus of roosters, all so certain
the sun will rise in just a few minutes.

Practice Problem

If I leave home at 12:48 PM, drive
8 miles, catch a plane accelerating
at 3 m/s² against the earth spinning
900 mph clockwise, and count

76 Royal palms from the sky before
I land in Havana at exactly 3:28 PM,
if I take a bus through rain falling
at 15° and cross a 1500-foot bridge

between two mountains where
my mother was born at 6:52 AM,
if I get off the bus, head south
at 36 mph in a '57 Buick with a tail

wind blowing off the sugarcane
south by southeast at 18 ft/s
to my grandfather's town where
I see the same 4,701 stars he saw

above his house, if I suddenly
decelerate at 2 m/s² to follow
a man in a straw hat for a mile
because he looks like my father,

if I turn around, walk 3,200 steps
per day, how long will it take me
to get back home knowing I have
1.2 billion seconds left to live?

El Florida Room

Not a study or a den, but *El Florida*
as my mother called it, a pretty name
for the room with the prettiest view
of the lipstick-red hibiscus puckered up
against the windows, the tepid breeze
laden with the brown-sugar scent
of loquats drifting in from the yard.

Not a sunroom, but where the sun
both rose and set, all day the shadows
of banana trees fan-dancing across
the floor, and if it rained, it rained
the loudest, like marbles plunking
across the roof under constant threat
of coconuts ready to fall from the sky.

Not a sitting room, but *El Florida,* where
I sat alone for hours with butterflies
frozen on the polyester curtains
and faces of Lladró figurines: sad angels,
clowns, and princesses with eyes glazed
blue and gray, gazing from behind
the glass doors of the wall cabinet.

Not a TV room, but where I watched
Creature Feature as a boy, clinging
to my brother, safe from vampires
in the same sofa where I fell in love
with Clint Eastwood and my Abuelo

watching westerns, or pitying women
crying in telenovelas with my Abuela.

Not a family room, but the room where
my father twirled his hair while listening
to eight-tracks of Elvis, read Nietzsche
and Kant a few months before he died,
where my mother learned to dance alone
as she swept, and I learned *salsa* pressed
against my Tía Julia's enormous breasts.

At the edge of the city, in the company
of crickets, beside the empty clothesline,
telephone wires, and the moon, tonight
my life is an old friend sitting with me
not in the living room, but in the light
of *El Florida*, as quiet and necessary
as any star shining above it.

Sitting on My Mother's Porch in Westchester, Florida

In the afternoon I see myself at night
through the hibiscus chasing fireflies
with my dead father who traps them
in glass jars—nightlights for my room.
It's always summer in the front yard:
my brother and I slicing watermelons
with grandfather's machete, our shirts
stained pink, mouths sticky with sugar
washed off as we play with the hose.
The gardenia my mother planted
twenty years ago blooms for the first time
again, while father still mows the lawn,
the grass clippings green glitter stuck
to the sweat on his hairy chest, his skin
the scent of yellow, of the sun ripening
heart-shaped mangos my grandmother
turns into marmalade to fatten me up.
Everything I am is here still, sitting
with my grandfather on lawn chairs
watching plum sunsets and the clouds
of his *tabaco* vanishing into the wind,
into the chirp of crickets echoing back
from stars that haven't moved since
I first saw them, and the moon not yet
replaced by the glow of the city's lights,
and the banyan tree across the street
as if never cut down, its shadow still
a cloud on the yard, dropping roots
as thick as my legs from its branches,

through the air, deep into the earth
here, for the rest of my life.

He's the man and I'm the girl, Beba,
though I'm not supposed to be.
We live in *Poghsquishy*, in New York
where my cousin is from. It's pretty
and snows a lot up there, like he says.
My room is the house with a pink roof,
the most biggest one on Cucamonga Street.
I make Pepín pancakes on the dresser
and strawberry Pop-Tarts in the lamp.
I give him a kiss just like my mom does
to my dad and he goes to work like him
in a *gigan'ic* building in the living room.
But he ain't got a car. He drives a horse
named *Charlie Horse* with purple spots.
Our son's name is Succotash, he barks,
licks Pepín's fingers when he gets home.
Hi sweetheart, I make him say and kiss me
like on the black-and-white TV shows.
He wants to cook us dinner; I tell him no
he can't—only the girl is supposed to.
How come? Just 'cause, that's all I say
and go into the kitchen in the closet,
come out with cups of Kool-Aid wine,
slices of blue and red Play-Doh pizza.
It's *deewishes,* but Succotash won't eat.
I yell at him like my grandmother does:
Sit up like a man! Eat or no dessert for you!
Succotash runs away—he's a big sissy.
Pepín is tired. We brush our teeth

with my pencils and jump into bed.
I turn off the lights like he asks me.
I ain't afraid of the dark or his eyes,
or when I put his arm around me.
Good night, honey, I say, give him a kiss
on the lips just like in the soap operas,
but he doesn't say nothing. He likes it
when we play house, hates it when
my dad comes in my room, real angry:
Who you talking to? What's going on?

I'm a boy who hates being a boy who loves cats and paint-by-number sets. She's a witch who loves being a witch who hates mortals. Every afternoon she pops in on channel six on top of a lamp shade or a banister, and I disappear behind the locked door of my bedroom. I paint my fingernails crayon-red, wrap a towel around my head like her bouffant, tie my sheets around my chest into a chiffon muumuu just like hers, the bedspread draped over my shoulders like her mauve cape. We give *Derwood* cat-eye scowls and scoff at Samantha's patience with mortals. In our raspy voices we cast spells turning Mrs. Kravitz into a Chihuahua and the boys at recess into ants I can squish. With a flick of our wrists we puncture the milkman's truck tires and conjure up thunderstorms to rain out baseball practice. With a wave of our billowy sleeves we give Larry Tate amnesia and trick my mother into signing me up for art classes. We brew bat's wings with eyes of newt into potions to make me like girls and my father a little more. We turn my grandmother into a mute so she can't scream me: *Go play outside! Don't be such a sissy! Talk like a man, will you?* For thirty minutes we sit on clouds, drink bubbly brews from cognac glasses, gaze into a crystal ball at my wonderful future until—poof—she disappears in a cloud of smoke, leaving me alone in my room again, the boy afraid of being a boy, dressed like a witch, wanting to vanish too.

Queer Theory: According to My Grandmother

Never drink soda with a straw—
    milk shakes? Maybe.
Stop eyeing your mother's Avon catalog,
and the men's underwear in those Sears flyers.
    I've seen you . . .
Stay out of her Tupperware parties
and perfume bottles—don't let her kiss you,
    she kisses you much too much.
Avoid hugging men, but if you must,
    pat them real hard
    on the back, even
    if it's your father.
Must you keep that cat? Don't pet him so much.
    Why don't you like dogs?
Never play house, even if you're the husband.
Quit hanging with that Henry kid, he's too pale,
    and I don't care what you call them
    those GI Joes of his
    are dolls.
Don't draw rainbows or flowers or sunsets.
    I've seen you . . .
Don't draw at all—no coloring books either.
Put away your crayons, your Play-Doh, your Legos.
    Where are your Hot Wheels,
    your laser gun and handcuffs,
    the knives I gave you?
Never fly a kite or roller skate, but light
    all the firecrackers you want,
    kill all the lizards you can, cut up worms—
    feed them to that cat of yours.

Don't sit *Indian* style with your legs crossed—
    you're no Indian.
Stop click-clacking your sandals—
    you're no girl.
For God's sake, never pee sitting down.
    I've seen you . . .
Never take a bubble bath or wash your hair
with shampoo—shampoo is for women.
    So is conditioner.
    So is mousse.
    So is hand lotion.
Never file your nails or blow-dry your hair—
go to the barber shop with your grandfather—
    you're not *unisex.*
Stay out of the kitchen. Men don't cook—
they eat. Eat anything you want, except:
    deviled eggs
    Blow Pops
    croissants (Bagels? Maybe.)
    cucumber sandwiches
    petit fours
Don't watch *Bewitched* or *I Dream of Jeannie.*
Don't stare at *The Six-Million Dollar Man.*
    I've seen you . . .
Never dance alone in your room:
Donna Summer, Barry Manilow, the Captain
and Tennille, Bette Midler, and all musicals—
    forbidden.
Posters of kittens, *Star Wars*, or the Eiffel Tower—
    forbidden.

Those fancy books on architecture and art—
      I threw them in the trash.
You can't wear cologne or puka shells
and I better not catch you in clogs.
If I see you in a ponytail—I'll cut it off.
What? No, you can't pierce your ear,
      left or right side—
      I don't care—
you will not look like a goddamn queer,
      I've seen you . . .
even if you are one.

Abuelo in a Western

A stranger steps into our Florida room,
glaring at Abuelo and me on the couch.
He shoots a man in the gut, then spits.
A real hombre, Abuelo says. The stranger

speaks mostly with his eyes, his gun,
shoots another man, punches another.
He never misses or loses, unlike Abuelo,
who misses his farm, his only brother,
and *his* Cuba, all lost to the revolution.

The stranger meets a woman, pins her
against a barrel. She pushes back but
then kisses him—he leaves her crying.
He can have any women he wants

but doesn't need a woman, like Abuelo,
who still holds my grandmother's hand
down the supermarket aisle, dances slow
on New Year's Eve with her. The stranger
doesn't have a wife, a home. He doesn't

watch tv like me and Abuelo, who lets me
rest my head on his lap while he scratches
my back, goose bumps daze my body limp.
He carries me to bed, kisses my forehead,

and leaves me in the dark, goes back
to the stranger, the hall echoing with more

bottles breaking, chairs smashing, women
screaming, shots that won't let me sleep—
Abuelo is nothing like that stranger, is he?

The Port Pilot

Before I knew him as a butcher
coming home with bloodstains
on his cuffs that Mamá could never
wash out in the kitchen sink, before

I learned he'd spend all day in the sky
in loafers and a necktie, counting
other people's money in a tower
with a view he couldn't afford, years

before he started gambling with me
on cockfights at Tío Burili's farm
every Saturday night, teaching me
how to bet on death, long before

he was diagnosed and staying alive
became his full-time job, his agenda
filled with appointments to kill
whatever was killing him, a lifetime

before I had to cradle him in and out
of bed, he carried me on his shoulders
over the jetty at the port, minutes after
I'm called to the hospital, I remember

that day: sitting together on a rock
watching the ships glide past us, when
he told me that years before he was
my father, he was a port pilot in Havana

steering ships safely into harbor, then
guiding them out to sea again, never
to see them again, seconds before I hear
his last breath, told to leave the room.

My Brother on Mt. Barker

As I write these lines he is somewhere
gilding down the mountain, and I'm here
on the ground. Funny, that's the way
it's always been: me looking up at him
conquering mountains, secretly wishing
I could be as daring as he, less like me.
Ten winters and I still haven't learned
how to ski, and yet there he is, a man
from Florida, weaving through slopes—
forever the athlete defying gravity—
and me, feet on the ground, asking what
makes us brothers. Blood is not enough
to explain this handful of memories
tethering us back to the years we took
building that village train set, and the day
we set it on fire in the backyard, because
we could, because we wanted to watch
how the world we created could burn.

Or maybe we've not been brothers at all
until this morning when I see him cross
his skis and tumble down to me, then
get up and dust the snow off his jacket.
Damn, my bones are killing me, he tells me
and I realize he doesn't know how to ski
that good, maybe he doesn't know much
more than I do about what makes living
worth falling. Suddenly I feel I should
tell him everything is going to be all right:

that he's still young, handsome enough
to find a another wife unlike the first,
that Lucas and Dominic will learn to live
in two homes, keep loving him more
than we could ever love our father.
But I know he doesn't need me to say
such things, so I don't. He needs me
to believe them silently, the same way
I need him to believe someday, maybe
next year, I'll learn how to ski and we
will glide down the mountain, together.

Papá at the Kitchen Table

my father moved through dooms of love
through sames of am through haves of give
—ee cummings

This isn't from a photograph of my father,
there's nothing to prove I remember him
like this: alone at the kitchen table beside
a crystal bowl dulled with plastic red grapes,
the curtains thin as vellum hung against
the morning light, holding back the sun
not yet risen above our terra-cotta rooftop.

And yet, I'll be driving on the interstate, or
mincing onions, or reading the newspaper,
when suddenly there he will be: the same
blue-striped boxers, his hairy legs crossed,
waiting for his espresso to brew, the glow
of the range, the glow of his cigarette—
tapping the ashes into the cup of his hand.

I can't remember any photo with his elbows
on the table, palms clasped around his face
like sepals of a flower, leaning into the light
of the window, seeing what I imagine he saw:
grackles squawking at nothing, the mangos
hanging like brick-red hearts, the sundial
shadows of light poles across the driveway.

Sometimes when I'm shaving he appears
in the mirror watching the thin, white film

of the moon in the morning sky vanishing
with the life I still wish for him, not the life
he had: fleeing Cuba to Madrid, ten dollars,
one suitcase, winter work at a bomb factory
in New York, then a butcher shop in Miami.

There's no snapshot of him head-bowed
to the floor, counting the terrazzo specks,
tugging at his eyebrows, thinking what I think
he thought: how he'd pay for my tuition,
a trip to Disney World he couldn't promise,
if he'd ever learn English, see Cuba again,
the gun I knew he kept under his bed.

Even though there's no black-and-white
to prove it, today as I walk the beach,
the sky, the sea, and my life are one
with his, the clouds stop and tell me
it's all true: the kitchen table, the aroma
of his espresso—black—the beams of light
piercing him, his eyes quiet and heavy
moonstones wishing me a good morning.

My Father, My Hands

My father gave me these hands, fingers
inch-wide and muscular like his, the same
folds of skin like squinted eyes looking
back at me whenever I wash my hands
in the kitchen sink and remember him
washing garden dirt off his, or helping
my mother dry the dishes every night.

These are his fingernails—square, flat—
ten small mirrors I look into and see him
signing my report card, or mixing batter
for our pancakes on Sunday mornings.
His same whorls of hair near my wrists,
magnetic lines that pull me back to him
tying my shoelaces, pointing at words
as I learned to read, and years later:
greasy hands teaching me to change
the oil in my car, immaculate hands
showing me how to tie my necktie.

These are his knuckles—rising, falling
like hills between my veins—his veins,
his pulse at my wrist under the watch
he left for me ticking since his death,
alive when I hold another man's hand
and remember mine around his thumb
through the carnival at Tamiami Park,
how he lifted me up on his shoulders,
his hands wrapped around my ankles
keeping me steady above the world, still.

Love as if Love

Before I dared kiss a man, I kissed
Elizabeth. Before I was a man, I was
twenty-three and she was thirty-five,
a woman old enough to know songs
I didn't—and that we wouldn't last
beyond the six weeks spent drinking
sweet German wine off our lips,
candles burning and music lifting
off the black vinyl, easing the taboo
between us, barefoot and sprawled
on blankets over her studio floor.

She played The Mamas & The Papas,
Holiday, and Carole King, closed my eyes
with her fingers until the notes broke
in my palms and the room filled up
with the flicker of monarchs. She sang
her life to me in lyrics about running
like a river, about rain, fire. She sang
until I wasn't afraid of her loose hair,
the scent of lilacs creased in her neck,
her small bones in the space between
her breasts, until I dared undress her.

Before I ever took a man, I gave in
to Elizabeth by the tiny green lights
of her stereo glowing like fireflies,
the turntable a shiny black moon
spinning with the songs I still hear

on the radio—driving and singing
straight into clouds moving farther
and farther away, but never quite
vanishing, like those nights falling
asleep with her rooted in my arms,
loving her as if I could love her.

Maybe

for Craig

Maybe it was the billboards promising
paradise, maybe those fifty-nine miles
with your hand in mine, maybe my sexy
roadster, the top down, maybe the wind
fingering your hair, sun on your thighs
and bare chest, maybe it was just the ride
over the sea split in two by the highway
to Key Largo, or the idea of Key Largo.
Maybe I was finally in the right place
at the right time with the right person.
Maybe there'd finally be a house, a dog
named Chu, a lawn to mow, neighbors,
dinner parties, and you forever obsessed
with crossword puzzles and Carl Young,
reading in the dark by the moonlight,
at my bedside every night. Maybe. Maybe
it was the clouds paused at the horizon,
the blinding fields of golden sawgrass,
the mangrove islands tangled, inseparable
as we might be. Maybe I should've said
something, promised you something,
asked you to stay a while, maybe.

Cheers to Hyakutake

Everglades National Park
for Carlos

The last time humans saw the comet,
man hadn't learned to speak, you said,
and we talked about them—us—grunting
at the sky, drawing deer and their hands
over cave walls with blood and soot.
That's all they—we—could do against
all we didn't know 17,000 years ago.
Now look at us, I said, we've walked
on the moon, mapped our galaxy,
seen the edges of the universe—not bad.
We were good at *that* kind of talk, those
mysteries of time and space, remember?

You pointed the telescope and fiddled
with the knobs—Look, that's Sirius,
you told me, then asked if all the stars
had been named. Probably, I thought,
we've named everything: this swamp
called *River of Grass*, under moon shadows
of trees called cypress, watching the light
of insects named fireflies, and ghosts
of birds you said were ibis sleeping
in the branches until sunrise. Names—

even for what we couldn't see or quite
understand: joy, hate, love, jealousy.
We were no good at *that* kind of talk,
remember? We had no language for

those mysteries: two men consumed
with one another. Why did we want
to leave as much as we wanted to stay
all our lives talking about Einstein,
fractals, black holes, always the end
of time, never the end of us. No words

for that attraction/repulsion stronger
than both our wills. Instead we spoke
about double stars orbiting one another,
one day colliding, destroying themselves
in one dense mass of light, and we raised
our plastic cups of wine to Hyakutake,
its fiery tail tearing through the sky—
Cheers, you said, putting your arm
around my shoulder, We'll never see
anything like this again. Remember?

Thicker Than Country

A Cuban like me living in Maine? Well,
what the hell, Mark loves his native snow
and I don't mind it, really. I love icicles,
even though I still decorate the house
with seashells and starfish. Sometimes
I want to raise chickens and pigs, wonder
if I could grow even a small mango tree
in my three-season porch. But mostly,
I'm happy with hemlocks and birches
towering over the house, their shadows
like sundials, the cool breeze blowing
even in the summer. Sometimes I miss
the melody of Spanish, a little, and I play
Celia Cruz, dance alone in the basement.
Sometimes I miss the taste of white rice
with *picadillo*—so I cook, but it's never
as good as my mother's. I don't miss her
or the smell of her Cuban bread as much
as I should. Most days I wonder why, but
when Mark comes home like an astronaut
dressed in his ski clothes, or I spy him
planting petunias in the spring, his face
smudged with this earth, or barbequing
in the summer when he asks me if I want
a *hamberg* or a *cheezeberg* as he calls them—
still making me laugh after twelve years—
I understand why the mountains here
are enough, white with snow or green
with palms, mountains are mountains,
but love is thicker than any country.

Killing Mark

His plane went down over Los Angeles
last week (again), or was it Long Island?
Boxer shorts, hair gel, his toothbrush
washed up on the shore at New Haven,
but his body never recovered, I feared.

Monday, he cut off his leg chain sawing—
bled to death slowly while I was shopping
for a new lamp, never heard my messages
on his cell phone: *Where are you? Call me!*
I told him to be careful. He never listens.

Tonight, fifteen minutes late, I'm sure
he's hit a moose on Route 26, but maybe
he survived, someone from the hospital
will call me, give me his room number.
I'll bring his pajamas, some magazines.

5:25: still no phone call, voice mail full.
I turn on the news, wait for the report:
flashes of moose blood, his car mangled,
as I buzz around the bedroom dusting
the furniture, sorting the sock drawer.

Did someone knock? I'm expecting
the sheriff by six o'clock. *Mr. Blanco,
I'm afraid . . .* he'll say, hand me a Ziploc
with his wallet, sunglasses, wristwatch.
I'll invite him in, make some coffee.

6:25: I'll have to call his mom, explain,
arrange to fly the body back. Do I have
enough garbage bags for his clothes?
I *should* keep his ties—but his shoes?
Order flowers—roses—white or red?

By seven-thirty I'm taking mental notes
for his eulogy, suddenly adorning all
I've hated, ten years worth of nose hairs
in the sink, of lost car keys, of chewing
too loud and hogging the bedsheets,

when Joey yowls, ears to the sound
of footsteps up the drive, and darts
to the doorway. I follow with a scowl:
Where the hell were you? Couldn't call?
Translation: *I die each time I kill you.*

Love Poem According to Quantum Theory
for Mark

According to theory, there's another
in an equal and opposite world who
dreams into words all I've never

captured in a handful of rain, a feather,
or palms swaying under a tarnished moon.
According to theory, there's another

who's growing younger as I grow older,
who'll remember what I'll forget soon:
every word, every poem, every letter

I've written—memories will wither
and disappear into that dark vacuum
where according to theory another

keeps embracing, kissing all the lovers
I've unembraced, unkissed, except you
with me in this world of words I'll never

find for us, yet always reaching farther
than Orion to where the stars all bloom,
and according to theory there's another
for you whose words are far more clever.

Birthday Portrait

Every time I look into my eyes hanging
on the wall of my mother's living room
I relive that morning: her dressing me
in my Mickey Mouse shirt still warm
from her iron, my white leather shoes—
the *good* ones—like two little moons
on my feet, my father's black comb
in her hand fussing with my cowlicks,
dabbing my hair with *Agua de Violetas*,
parting it over and over until perfect.

I recall the long drive to the *big* Sears,
the tall racks of dresses and trousers
I couldn't see over as I followed her
through the store to some strange lady
who picked me up, plopped me down
before a frightful man in a red top hat,
a mean puppet in his hand, ordering me:
look at the camera, the birdie—smile, smile,
and then my mother: *smile, mi'jo, smile,*
then the crowd: *smile—come on—smile.*

But I didn't. I couldn't. I stared coldly
through everyone into a world far away
from the scent of violets, my perfect hair,
the Mickey Mouse smiling on my shirt.
Was I scared? Did I know something
I shouldn't have? That I can't remember,
still don't know what to answer myself

every time I look into my eyes, hanging
in my mother's living room asking me:
Why have you been sad all your life?

Mamá with Indians: 1973, 2007

I thought Mamá could never die, then
I saw her—right there—in full color
captured by two Indians, their faces
streaked with blood, one wielding
a tomahawk above her, the other a spear
inches away from her neck, her mouth
frozen in a scream that wouldn't stop
trembling in my hand. I peeled the photo
from the album, hid it in my drawer,
daring a peek every night at bedtime.
How could this be—

      there aren't any Indians
in Miami? Who saved her—Papá?
Where was I? I questioned silently
for days, until I saw the Indians' eyes
had no pupils, their skin was too shiny,
their weapons too dull—like plastic.
Then I found a door in the prairie sky
painted behind the stuffed buffalo,
a twinkle in Mamá's *not-so-scared* eyes,
and I put the photo back, believing
once again she would live

      forever, but now
she forgets names, doesn't sew or talk
about my father much anymore, today
I found her tossing his shoes and boxes
of old photos, hobbling on her bad knee

until it hurt and she had to take her throne—
the faded La-Z-Boy with gashed armrests
she won't replace: *This one will outlive me,*
she chuckles, and I see the Indians again
surrounding her, knowing this time she
might not escape—and I can't save her.

Venus in Miami Beach

What calls her to the sea? She rises, steps
toward the shore with the temperament
of a bride, her shadow a long train pulled
across the sand behind her, parting a flock
of seagulls screeching away into the wind.

Her swollen ankles and frail shoulders
disappear inch by inch under her body
as she wades into the water, becoming
as young as I remember her in a photo
posing like a mermaid for my father.

Once, as gorgeous as her name—*Geysa*—
once a girl chasing fireflies who hadn't lost
her home and country, sisters and husband,
once a mother who watched me as I watch
her now, afraid of her alone with the sea.

I wave to her, but she turns away from me,
fixes her eyes on the horizon and beyond
at nothing I can see, needing no one
it seems, like Venus's gaze I'm tempted
to think, born full-grown out of the sea.

But today, she's not a goddess or a girl,
not my mother, but simply a *her*, floating
in the circle of her own arms, a water lily,
tranquil and sure of her being, being.

Cooking with Mamá in Maine

Two years since trading mangos
for these maples, the white dunes
of the beach for the White Mountains
etched in my living room window,
I ask my mother to teach me how
to make my favorite Cuban dish.

She arrives from Miami in May
with a parka and plantains packed
in her suitcase, chorizos, *vino seco*,
but also onions, garlic, olive oil
as if we couldn't pick these up
at Hannaford's in Oxford County.

She brings with her all the spices
of my childhood: laurel, *pimentón*,
dashes of memories she sprinkles
into a black pot of black beans
starting to simmer when I wake up
and meet her busy in the kitchen.

With my pad and pencil eager
to take notes, I ask her how many
teaspoons of cumin, of oregano,
cups of oil, vinegar, she's adding,
but I can't get a straight answer:
I don't know, she says, *I just know.*

Afraid to stay in the guest cottage,
by herself, but not of the blood

on her hands, she stabs holes
in the raw meat, stuffs in garlic:
*Six or seven mas ó menos, maybe
seven cloves*, she says, *it all depends.*

She dices *about* one bell pepper,
tells me how much my father loved
her cooking too, as she cries over
about two onions she chops, tosses
into a pan sizzling with olive oil
making *sofrito* to brown the roast.

She insists I just watch her hands
stirring, folding, whisking me back
to the kitchen I grew up in, dinner
for six of us on the table, six sharp
every day of her life for thirty years
until she had no one left to cook for.

I don't ask how she survived her *exilio*:
ten years without her mother, twenty
as a widow. Did she grow to love snow
those years in New York before Miami,
and how will I survive winters here with
out her cooking? Will I ever learn?

But she answers every question when
she raises the spoon to my mouth saying,
Taste it, mi'jo, there's no recipe, just taste.

House of the Virgin Mary
Ephesus, Turkey

There have been no miracles here: no
wall lined with abandoned crutches or
offerings of roses browning in the sun
left by the once blind or the once dying,
no robed apparitions making promises
to any children or peasants wandering
these fields, in fact there is some doubt
whether she lived here at all. It is difficult
to imagine the mother of a savior living
in such a simple house of hewn stones,
a sentinel of cypress pines guarding her
quietly spending the last years of her life
among the silent bows of the olive trees,
cooking meals in the hearth day after day,
carrying water from the trickling spring
that must have sounded exactly the same
two thousand years ago, before basilicas
were built for her, before pilgrims crawled
on bloody knees to kneel before her gaze
and kiss her bare feet chiseled in marble.

~

Only the stones, the pines, the spring
can know for sure if she lived here once.
Still, I light a candle at the votive stand,
not because I believe this place is sacred,
or because I was Joseph in the fifth-grade
Nativity play, not because Sister Pancretila
assured me she *was* the mother of God, but

simply because she was, after all, a mother.
Gazing into the tiny flames I imagine her
sorrow: Did she miss Jerusalem or forget
herself in this foreign land? Did she ever
stop grieving her son, or ever find peace
in these hills, accept all that was as meant
to be—*now and at the hour of her death?*

~

I walk down the flagstone path knowing
someday my mother will die and I too
will walk through her house imagining
her thoughts those years she lived alone:
how many times might she have paused
in the doorway of the bedroom where
she held my dying father for the last time,
or sit at the kitchen table where she read
the telegram from Cuba announcing
her mother's death? How many times
did she think of replacing the furniture
in my old bedroom, or fall asleep alone
in the Florida room? How many nights
did she lie in bed staring at the threads
of the window sheers in the moonlight,
praying the rosary, mother to mother,
woman to woman, waiting for a miracle,
or giving thanks forever and ever amen?

Mi Rosa y Mi Sal
for Sonia

Some years ago I took four rose petals
flat on a board, sprinkled them with salt,
preserving their color as my gift to her:
Eres mi rosa y mi sal, I wrote on the back.

Flat and sprinkled with salt, the board
still hangs on a wall inside her studio.
Mi rosa, I read, *mi sal,* and think back
to the nights she filled with *salsa* music,

hanging out in her studio, the walls
listening to her chitchat about *la vida*
as we danced *salsa*, filling the night
with whatever she wanted to believe.

Through chitchat, I learned of her life:
the deadbeat husband, drugs in Harlem—
and I wanted to believe as she believed:
Depués de todo, la vida sigue bella, she'd say—

Life keeps beautiful after all, she still says,
the four rose petals just as red as the day
I gave them to her, sprinkled with salt.

Questioning My Cousin Elena

I'm sure somewhere there's a photo
of me sitting on your lap mesmerized
by your false eyelashes like giant black
butterflies opening, closing. Surely
you had neon-green daisies painted
on your bedroom walls, every song
of the Beatles on 45s. Where is
that lemon-yellow T-shirt I loved
on you, the smiley face stretched
across your breasts? It's true, isn't it—
you teased your hair and once I took
a taste of it thinking it was frosting?

I must remember you right: a big-city,
gum-smacking girl from the Big Apple
who said *wauter* not *water.* You wore
white vinyl boots up to your knees
and miniskirts parading yourself
and me alongside down Riverside
pretending I was your firstborn.
If I remember the Hudson's gray,
surely I remember us ten years later
cool as your Camaro slicing through
the shadows of palm trees in Miami,
you teaching me the words to that song
about silly love songs on the radio.
I remember the lyrics, don't you?

I haven't put words in your mouth,
or in my mind, have I? You did say

it was love you wanted and not God
when you began dressing in white
and chanting to the spirits of Yoruba.
You did adore your father in his recliner,
a 20-cent cigar, a can of Schlitz praising
you as too smart for your own good.
You still miss him, don't you? Tell me
it's true, we're everything we remember,
tell me memories never fail us, tell me
we take them with us, that I'll take you
with me, and you'll take me with you.

In a pleated skirt and pearl choker, dusted
with perfumed talc, dressed for company,
not like this: wearing a threadbare housecoat
pitched over the ends of her bones, sinking
into the sofa, smiling without her dentures,
remembering nothing
                              I remember about her:
not her old apartment in Little Havana, nor
her knitted doilies like snowflakes dressing
the tears on her vinyl sofa, nor the buttons
like eyes, not the glassy eyes on her statuette
of San Lázaro, not his 14K halo, nor the gold
rimmed cups, not the *café* she'd serve in them,
not the *caldo gallego* she'd cook for my father
after his chemotherapy,
                              nor my father, none
of her recipes for *tasajo* and *fricasé de pollo*, nor
the taste of tomatoes, cumin, the mangos
from her husband's orchard back in Cuba, not
even her husband, nor the island she swore
she'd never forget, not the stories she told me
of peanut vendors singing, fireflies dancing
in Parque Palmira,
                              not the park, the street
she lived on, the names of her neighbors, nor
the name of her daughter, now feeding her
black bean *potaje*, asking her if she knows
her own name, if she knows who I am. *No,*

she shakes her head, terrifying me that a life
can come to an end like this:
                              every memory
one by one slipped out of her body, her cells,
until she never was, like a movie rewinding,
ending on a blank screen, like petals closing
back into a bud, or a broken string of pearls
skipping across the floor, like a wave drunk
by the sand or clouds thinning back to air,
a raindrop returned to the sea, the reflection
of the sky in a puddle lifting back into sky.

Unspoken Elegy for Tía Cucha

I arrive with a box of guava *pastelitos*,
a dozen red carnations, and a handful
of memories at her door: the half-moons
of her French manicures, how she spoke
blowing out cigarette smoke, her words
leaving her mouth as ghosts, the music
of her nicknames: *Cucha, Cuchita, Pucha*.
I kiss her hello and she slaps me hard
across my arm: *¡Cabrón! Too handsome
to visit your Tía, eh?* She laughs, pulls me
inside her efficiency, a place I thought
I had forgotten, comes back to life
with wafts of Jean Naté and Pine Sol,
the same calendar from *Farmacia León*
with scenes of Old Havana on the wall,
the same peppermints in a crystal dish.
And her, wearing a papery housecoat,
sneakers with panty hose, like she wore
those summer mornings she'd walk me
down to the beach along First Street,
past the washed-out pinks and blues
of the Art Deco hotels like old toys.
The retirees lined across the verandas
like seagulls peering into the horizon,
the mango popsicles from the *bodeguita*
and the pier she told me was once
a bridge to Cuba—have all vanished.

I ask how she's feeling, but we agree
not to talk about *that* today, though

we both know why I have come
to see her: in a few months, maybe
weeks, her lungs will fill up again,
her heart will stop for good. She too
will vanish, except what I remember
of her, this afternoon: sharing a *pastelito*,
over a *café* she sweetens with Equal
at her dinette table crowded with boxes
of low-salt saltines and fibery cereals.
Under the watch of Holy Jesus' heart
burning on the wall, we gossip about
the secret crush she had on my father
once, she counts exactly how many
years and months since she left Cuba
and her mother forever. We complain
about the wars, disease, fires blazing
on the midday news as she dunks
the flowers in a tumbler—a dozen red
suns burst in the sapphire sky framed
in the window, sitting by the table.

Bones, Teeth

His bones, his teeth. Does hair decay? I ask
myself as I watch my mother on her knees
pouring water over my father's gravestone,
her palm gently washing the bronze letters
as if she were stroking his face once again.

With school scissors, she cuts the blades
of grass from the edges, yanks the weeds
creeping underneath the Crown of Thorns,
still alive ten years since she planted it
in the dirt that is my father now, forever.

His wedding band, cuff links, bones, teeth—
that's probably all that's left of him here,
I tell myself as she replaces the dead
mums with a dozen fresh ones that'll last
only a few days in the sun, she complains.

Her eyes fixed on the ground, she speaks
silently with him, feeling what I cannot:
the haunt of his breath, his touch rising
from deep inside the earth that waits
for her also, beside him again, someday.

Who will tend his grave when she's gone
too? I worry, suddenly thinking of winters
driving past old cemeteries, gravestones
under snowdrifts, the dead and their dead
children and grandchildren—forgotten.

Where will I be buried? There's no place
for me here. Who'll visit with flowers,
speak to what's left of me? Yet I won't
kiss his grave. Forgive me, Papá, bones
that are my bones, teeth that are my teeth.

Burning in the Rain

Someday compassion would demand
I set myself free of my desire to recreate
my father, indulge in my mother's losses,
strangle lovers with words, forcing them
to confess for me and take the blame.
Today was that day: I tossed them, sheet
by sheet on the patio and gathered them
into a pyre. I wanted to let them go
in a blaze, tiny white dwarfs imploding
beside the azaleas and ficus bushes,
let them crackle, burst like winged seeds,
let them smolder into gossamer embers—
a thousand gray butterflies in the wind.
Today was that day, but it rained, kept
raining. Instead of fire, water—drops
knocking on doors, wetting windows
into mirrors reflecting me in the oaks.
The garden walls and stones swelling
into ghostlier shades of themselves,
the wind chimes giggling in the storm,
a coffee cup left overflowing with rain.
Instead of burning, my pages turned
into water lilies floating over puddles,
then tiny white cliffs as the sun set,
finally drying all night under the moon
into papier-mâché souvenirs. Today
the rain would not let their lives burn.

Place of Mind

Mist haunts the city, tears of rain fall
from the awnings and window ledges.
The search for myself begins an echo
drifting away the moment I arrive.

From the awnings and window ledges
follow the rain flowing down the streets.
The moment I arrive, I drift away:
Why am I always imagining the sea?

Follow the rain flowing down the streets
vanishing into the mouths of gutters.
Why am I always imagining the sea?
A breath, a wave—a breath, a wave.

Vanishing into the mouths of gutters,
rain becomes lake, river, ocean again.
A breath, a wave—a breath, a wave
always beginning, yet always ending.

Rain becomes lake, river, ocean, again
mist haunts the city, tears of rain fall.
Always ending, yet always beginning,
the search for myself ends in echo.

Some Days the Sea

The sea is never the same twice. Today
the waves open their lions' mouths hungry
for the shore, and I feel the earth helpless.
Some days their foamy edges are lace
at my feet, the sea a sheet of green silk.
Sometimes the shore brings souvenirs
from a storm, I sift spoils of sea grass:
find a broken finger of coral, a torn fan,
examine a sponge's hollow throat, watch
a man-of-war die a sapphire in the sand.
Some days there's nothing but sand
quiet as snow, I walk, eyes on the wind
sometimes laden with silver-tasting salt,
sometimes still as the sun. Some days
the sun is a dollop of honey and raining
light on the sea glinting diamond dust,
sometimes there are only clouds, clouds—
sometimes solid as continents drifting
across the sky, other times wispy, white
roses that swirl into tigers, into cathedrals,
into hands, and I remember some days

I'm still a boy on this beach, wanting
to catch a seagull, cup a tiny silver fish,
build a perfect sand castle. Some days I am
a teenager blind to death even as I watch
waves seep into nothingness. Most days
I'm a man tired of being a man, sleeping
in the care of dusk's slanted light, or a man

scared of being a man, seeing *some* god
in the moonlight streaming over the sea.
Some days I imagine myself walking
this shore with feet as worn as driftwood,
old and afraid of my body. Someday,
I suppose I'll return *someplace* like waves
trickling through the sand, back to sea
without any memory of being, but if
I could choose eternity, it would be here:
aging with the moon, enduring in the space
between every grain of sand, in the cusp
of every wave and every seashell's hollow.

Since Unfinished

I've been writing this since
the summer my grandfather
taught me how to hold a blade
of grass between my thumbs
and make it whistle, since
I first learned to make green
from blue and yellow, turned
paper into snowflakes, believed
a seashell echoed the sea,
and the sea had no end.

I've been writing this since
a sparrow flew into my class
and crashed into the window,
laid to rest on a bed of tissue
in a shoebox by the swings, since
the morning I first stood up
on the bathroom sink to watch
my father shave, since our eyes
met in that foggy mirror, since
the splinter my mother pulled
from my thumb, kissed my blood.

I've been writing this since
the woman I slept with the night
of my father's wake, since
my grandmother first called me
a faggot and I said nothing, since
I forgave her and my body

pressed hard against Michael
on the dance floor at Twist, since
the years spent with a martini
and men I knew couldn't love.

I've been writing this since
the night I pulled off the road
at Big Sur and my eyes caught
the insanity of the stars, since
the months by the kitchen window
watching the snow come down
like fallout from a despair I had
no word for, since I stopped
searching for a name and found
myself tick-tock in a hammock
asking nothing of the sky.

I've been writing this since
spring, studying the tiny leaves
on the oaks dithering like moths,
contrast to the eon-old fieldstones
unveiled of snow, but forever
works-in-progress, since tonight
with the battled moon behind
the branches spying on the world—
same as it ever was—perfectly
unfinished, my glasses and pen
at rest again on the night table.

I've been writing this since
my eyes started seeing less,
my knees aching more, since
I began picking up twigs, feathers,
and pretty rocks for no reason
collecting on the porch where
I sit to read and watch the sunset
like my grandfather did everyday,
remembering him and how
to make a blade of grass whistle.

Acknowledgments

Grateful acknowledgment is made to the editors of the following publications in which these poems first appeared, sometimes in earlier versions: *New Republic*: "Burning in the Rain"; *Packing-house Review*: "Betting on America" and "The Name I Wanted:"; *Pool*: "Taking My Cousin's Photo at the Statue of Liberty"; *Review: Literature and Arts of the Americas, no 78*: "El Florida Room," "Some Days the Sea," and "Unspoken Elegy for Tía Cucha"; *Divining Divas*: "Afternoons as Endora"; *MiPoesias*: "Looking for The Gulf Motel"; *Sugar House Review*: "Tía Margarita Johnson's House in Hollywood," "The Port Pilot," and "Venus in Miami Beach"; *Ocean State Review*: "Queer Theory: According to My Grandmother" and "Love as if Love"; *Floating Wolf Quarterly*: "Unspoken Elegy for Tía Cucha," "Of Consequence, Inconsequently," "Place of Mind," and "Some Days the Sea"; and *TriQuarterly*: "Cheers to Hyakutake."

I also thank *mis hermanos*: Brian Leung, Peter Covino, Stuart Bernstein, Fred Arroyo, Spencer Reece, John Bailly, and Francisco Aragón for their generosity as readers as well as their spiritual help with these poems. And as always, Mark, who makes it all worthwhile.